Sometimes – watching the n‹
or listening to the radio – it's
all over bar the shouting. We're
screwed. On our way to hell in a beautifully woven
handbasket with the only argument being whose cool
and edgy branding we spray onto the wickerwork and
how much the TV rights will rake in. We've been
beaten by trolls and grifters and power-hungry men
(and women) with bad hair, each and every one of
them absolutely certain of their own importance and
their place in history.

Well, mebbe.

I've never really been one for paying attention to what
I'm told. There's a poem or two about that in here. And
there are poems which celebrate our bitter-sweet,
beautiful lives, our hopes, our ridiculous dreams. Our
insistence on looking at the stars even when we're
lying in a post-industrial gutter. These are poems of
love and life and laughter, and I hope they make you
smile and put a small song in your heart. Just don't ask
me to sing it. Nobody needs that.

cheers

Steve

As mosquitos bring down monsters
with their numbers and persistence
we change the world by increments
with our love and our resistance

thirty-one small acts of love and resistance

Steve Pottinger

ISBN: 978-0-9932044-7-0

typeset by Steve at Ignite.
www.ignitebooks.co.uk

Printed and bound in the UK
by Bell & Bain Ltd,
Glasgow.

for everyone who does

Contents

many of the poems in this collection
have previously been published in anthologies,
or online

trainspotting, 1832
Kevin the machinist dodges natural history...
On the way to the shops...
were all commissioned by Multistory
for their 'Tipton Tales' project

the folk who read the news
features in the 'On Fighting On' anthology from
the Bread & Roses competition

top deck
is online as part of the 'Black Country' project

On hearing of the financial difficulties...
welcoming the brave new world...
universal credit *individual pain*
have all been published in the Morning Star

Desaparecida
was published online by Proletarian Poetry

Olives only once, mind...
is published as one of the Poetry on Loan
poetry postcards

Mothers' Day
was commended in the Prole poetry comp 2019

the drunken Polish labourer...
was runner-up in the same comp

after years of putting her down...
was previously published in the anthology
'Bollox to Brexit'.

Enough
and
In Which No.45 Once Again...
were both published online by Culture Matters

you do not listen
was published online by the International Times

Glass collector
was a winner in the 2018
Bread & Roses poetry competition

and for those of you who enjoy poetry videos...
the folk who read the news
and
impulse
can both be found on Youtube

trainspotting, 1832

So here's us, grafting away
mines, factories, furnaces
every which way you look

men, women, kids our work
turning the sky red by night
black as coal by day

making boats, rails, bridges
chains, nails, keys, all of it
with our sweat, our hands, our toil

dying in accidents and explosions
buried in pit falls and mass graves
someone new in our place by morning

and some of us stoke our anger
some say it's just the way it is
either way, it's us grafting

putting bread on the table
living hand to hungry mouth
been this way since Adam was a boy

then Victoria comes through by train
future queen of empire, she who'll have
us paint the world red in her honour

I admit, I was curious
what will we make of her?
what will she think of us?

will anything come of it?
will the royal eye survey
our kingdom, and feel pride?

her majesty's carriages never slowed
curtains drawn tight over windows
so as not to see us, the glow of hell

at her country's heart her gravediggers
her mineworkings, her people
and rage burned through me

I screamed at train and curtains
as they rolled into the distance
Sorry, your highness, for even existing!

then I spat on my hands
and I set back to work
trying to put food on the table

and it's us, grafting away
mines, factories, furnaces
every which way you look

men, women, kids, our work
turning the sky red by night
black as coal by day

the folk who read the news

the folk who read the news never look like us
you don't see them down the chippy
or queueing in line for the rush-hour bus
they don't drive vans, or work the tills,
or have hard hats on their head
but imagine things were different
and looked like this instead...
we wake up in a world where we switch on the TV
flick through all the channels and this is what we see:
a fella in a high-vis interviews the Minister for Health
while a lass on zero-hours quizzes a CEO on wealth
political correspondents fresh from stacking shelves
experts in their field who are the mirror of ourselves
language rich in dialect and accent
anchors of every shape and size
who mutter *bollocks* to the camera
when the Prime Minister tells lies
sports news brought into our living rooms
by kids off the estate
who know the subject backwards
*He ****ing dived! I tell, you, mate!*
pensioners from Blackpool
do the guide to entertainment
reports on poverty and foodbanks
by people formerly known as 'claimants'
who were anonymous and voiceless

but now have the platform to explain
how going cap-in-hand demeans
and we can do better than go there again
cut to a piece on childcare
and now it's time to get the weather
from a single mum in a B&B
who's holding it together
and who promises the cold snap
will soon be pushed away
by high pressure moving in from the Azores
smiles, and says who thought we'd see the day
when the folk who read the news
are people just like us
and we see them down the chippy
or queueing in line for the rush-hour bus.

top deck

from way up here, you can see it all

the terrible beauty
of pensioners staring through windows
schoolkids slouching towards the classroom
not wanting to go

you see
flashing lights at the level crossing
diesel running back to base, light loco
arctics moving stuff from there to here
inching in the nose-to-tail-to-nose

you see
the dumpy ballet of fork-lifts
the loading and unloading
men in the new flat cap of the company hi-vis
grafting and grousing and joking

you see
backyard mechanics in corrugated yards
smeared in oil and grease
the nodded *corsayfairer*
the sheen of puddles and of handshakes

you see
the lads on bikes
who have nothing to their names
yet pull perfect effortless wheelies
the length of their street day after day after day

you see
Johnny striding down the towpath
can of Special on the go
two more in his coat pocket
just to take the edge off, you know?

and in between the high-rise
where the sun glints through
you can sometimes see hope
if you squint real hard

and let your gaze slip out of focus

On hearing of the financial difficulties of a peddler of hate

This morning, you have forgone
the sullen trudge to work,
spring – two at a time – up bus stairs,
whistle as you settle into a seat
at the front with the world's best view.

The grey skies are wonderful,
the traffic a joy, one long beautiful
                    bless it!
bumper-to-bumper congestion
a symphony of horns
and humming engines.

The city has been washed brighter
overnight. You smile at strangers, cyclists,
policemen, wish chuggers a cheery good day
offer your breakfast pastry
to a figure curled in a shop doorway.

Cackling, you play hopscotch
the length of the high street,
vow to laugh at the boss's lame jokes.
                    Vow to try.

Some days, you tell yourself,
are truly magical. What times,
what times, what times to be alive!

Black Country lunch-break

You don't see the beauty
when you're looking at a map.
All this sprawl, these roads, this housing
looks forgettable and crap,
nowhere you'd want to choose to come
more somewhere you'd wash up.
But the place we work and rest and play?
It's here. It's home.

And this morning, the sun on my face,
me stepping outside to lean against the wall
and take a break from the heat of the press,
there were swifts overhead
the water in the cut as clear as crystal
coots, moorhens, a pair of swans,
flag iris by the fistful
reeds and birch all waving in the breeze.
I'm nothing special, a simple man
one of the just-about-managing
but moments like these,
they make my heart sing.

I drink it all in.
Water lilies and motorways
sprawl, solidarity, and roads
drag hard on the fag

I tell the wife I'm giving up
but you know how it goes.
I will. I should. I have, more or less.

Then I slip back in through the chain-link fence
to the rhythm and beat and the heat of the press.

Kevin the machinist dodges natural history and pops out for a pint

She's planned an evening
snuggled on the sofa
but Kevin's got a thirst on
and he's off down to the pub.
Friday evening, life's too short
for sitting watching telly
and chips and curry sauce
will do for him as grub.
As he walks he wonders
when will the cameras come to Tipton
Those folk who mek the progammes
– he shakes his head – *they'm saft*
get all worked up about Eskimos
just coz they've fifty words for snow.
Big deal. Film here, we'll learn you
how we've twenty-seven different languages

for graft.

On the way to the shops, a young mom finds a sudden interest in local history

Pushing Chantelle down Factory Road
she wonders what they made there.
Soap? Pork pies? Pig iron? Hats?
Leans forward over the stroller, whispers
Little uns, bab. We've always been good at that.

parkour

in another city
or another part of town
one of them would be filming this
on his Go-Pro
the slo-mo catching every leap,
the light just right,
camera passing over the designer brands
casually-worn because they know they deserve them
a montage of smiles and high-fives,
boyish bravado
set to a soundtrack of edgy music
by guitar bands too cool for you to know

here
it's just a gang of scallies
in trackies making a din
clambering up the scaffolding
shrieking at the top of their voices
calling each other *wankaaar!*
shattering the silence
of a sunday afternoon
like someone else's windows
raising a little bit of hell
before the rain returns
or recreation turns to need

or the cops roll in
too bored of this for sirens

doing the old dance
same as the new dance
same as the old dance
par for the course

a poem examining the sociological implications of an incident at Wolverhampton swimming baths where – as I slammed my locker shut – a bloke leaving the changing room swung his bag over his shoulder and his beanie fell to the floor behind him, an incident which I believe (without wishing to overstate the case in any way) offers hope to all humanity

I shouted *Oi! Fella! You've dropped your hat!*
and he said *Thanks, mate. I'd have lost that.*

this heat

and we peel off clothes without thinking
wear next to nothing, ride the breeze

sun spreading itself over skin like honey
the damp funk of bedsheets

sliding over the slick of you
lickingsaltsweatsweetness

finding my way to the heat of you
this heat, this incredible heat

Desaparecida

I did not know you.

I did not know you and I was not there
when Tuesday morning burst in upon you,
kicked down the doors and stormed
into the flat, when a dozen men with guns,
– *policia* doing the work of the cartel –
dragged you to the cars that waited,
idling outside, dance tunes on the radio,
drivers tapping their fingers, humming along.

I did not know you and I was not there
when they drove you to a nameless faceless place
built of breeze blocks, nightmares, fear
of hours that stretch forever
and the death of strangers
I was not there and when they did to you
what men with brutal minds and guns
have always done to women
I still didn't know you. I still wasn't there.

I did not know you and I was not there
when they set you free
when you stumbled back home
I was not there and I do not know
if you leant chairs against the broken door

to close out the world and its guns and its hate
I do not know if you curled up on the bed and sobbed
or stood under the shower for dripping hours
hoping to wash away hurt and sin and shame
I was not there when you sat at the table and shook
when you smoked one trembling cigarette after another
when you cursed the god who lets these men
– these *malditos culeros* – run free
when you prayed to our lady,
to anyone who'd listen.

I did not know you and I was not there
when they came back
when they came back
and took you away again
when the car waited, idling outside,
driver tapping his fingers, humming along
when they wrote your name in sand and blood
in the long long list of *desaparecidas*

I did not know you and I was not there
and it's not enough, it will never be enough
but I write this poem
to keep alive your name
to light a candle of words,
a small but steady flame
that burns bright in the howling dark
and remembers you.

Olives only once, mind...

Two years on, she sleeps
whichever side of the bed she wants,
spends money how she fancies.
Tries olives, cocktails, trampolines.
Visits an art gallery, paints a wall,
sits in the garden for hours
watching the light shift, change,
fade, fall. Sings in the bath,
the kitchen too, if the mood takes her.
Goes to the gym and the pub. Loves both.
Loves chips more. Is a woman
of appetite and smiles.
Apologises for nothing.

Doesn't think of him at all.

Mothers' Day

Let us sing a song of the tiny tattered town
of the pub at its locked-down, knocked-down heart
and of those who drink there.
Let us sing of Mothers' Day and celebration
of the family night out
of a large glass of red and the *make that a double*
of burgers with all the trimmings
a side of onion rings and chips with everything
sing of curry and a pint and change from a tenner.

Let us sing of the bevy of traveller women
loud and drinking and drunk
and their *don't care a toss if you serve food*
we're bringing the pizzas in anyway
don't think of stopping us nonchalance,
sing of their children
who climb barefoot over the tables
over and under and through
caring nothing for rules.

Let us sing of the bar-staff, budget-uniformed,
overworked and underpaid
who are suddenly busy at the other end of the bar
who have a finely tuned instinct for looking
the other way
who know there's not a chance in the world

the money covers this, no chance at all.
Let us sing of it being someone else's problem
quite definitely someone else's problem.

Let us sing, then, of the young manager
his stooped shoulders, his muttering, his sighs
as he wanders over for the third time
counting the minutes, praying to get to
the end of the shift without it kicking off,
sing of the token gesture of negotiation
sing of putting to one side the memory
of what happened last time.
Sing of his hope he doesn't have to draw the line.

Let us sing of everyone in there
knowing the cops will be late, useless
sing of keeping one eye on the exit
of knowing that if it all goes down
well, devil take the hindmost.
Let us sing of take a deep breath and bear it
of it not being your business, none of it
of swallowing this down, of letting it slide.

Let us sing of hours measured pint by pint
of old men slipping home
of the crackling tension of trouble ebbing
like a tide you hadn't noticed turn.
Let us sing of lost nights, last buses,

of *just one more before you go*
of pizza crusts trodden in carpets
of traveller women, beyond drunk now,
queens of all they can keep in focus.

Let us sing, my friends.
Sing a song of the tiny, tattered town
of the pub at its locked-down, knocked-down heart
and of those who drink there.
Let us sing of Mothers' Day and celebration
of the family night out
of empty glasses and a last one for the road.
Let us raise our cracked and tuneless voices
and let us sing.

welcoming the brave new world of this positive mentality

this morning, embracing the spirit
of a newly energised nation
Kevin is at the foodbank once more
giddy with what he knows now
must be enthusiasm
which he – fool that he is –
had mistaken for hunger

believing in himself and what he can achieve
he picks tins of can-do beans
from the shelf – a small step, yes
but one he understands will lead
sure as eggs is eggs
to a better future

later, he will skip happily
through sunlit uplands
singing hallelujahs to the landlord
for renting out a flat with no room
for self-doubt, negativity,

or swinging the cat
he's not allowed under the terms
of his agreement.

universal credit   *individual pain*

this system is transforming people's lives
                    I lived off cereal, so the kids could eat
it's helping them into work and it's working for them
                    I went in my room in a sleeping bag
                    and stayed there for two weeks
it's a great example of British innovation
                    yesterday, I had two pieces of toast;
                    the day before, two drop scones
based on leading-edge technology
and agile working practices
                    I'm going to go upstairs
                    and slit my wrists
our strategy is based on continuous improvement
                    we just won't be able to pay the rent
you are a person who must be treated
as not in Great Britain
                    where am I then?
                    I've lived here since I was nine
you do not have any entitlement
to Universal Credit at this time
                    I'm sick of arguing with these people,
                    I'm sick of arguing on the phone
we are leading the world,
we are leading the world
                    we've gone back to the 18th century,
                    they're living in cuckoo land

a poem examining the sociological implications of an incident at Wolverhampton swimming baths where – as I slammed my locker shut – a bloke leaving the changing room swung his bag over his shoulder and his beanie fell to the floor behind him, an incident which I believe (without wishing to overstate the case in any way) offers hope to all humanity (revisited)

I didn't think to check his politics
ask if he preferred The Clash over The Fall
if he was a closet egg-chaser
or had the usual soft spot for wendyball
I didn't broach that bloody Brexit
or ask him what he thought
of the perennial problem of supply and demand
or if he just enjoyed the pictures in the Daily Sport
I didn't ask, even in passing
for his take on the new Gillette ad
the old bill
or ancient history
I didn't seek out his opinion on
the rat race
the human race

the space race
or if he held out any realistic hope
of intelligent life being found on Piers Morgan
I know it's remiss but I'll own up to this:
I never even asked if he supported Villa.
I didn't enquire whether he liked sausage rolls of pork
or would rather they were vegan
or if he was a fan of Bjork
and where the hell has she gone?
I assumed the hi-vis in his rucksack
showed he was heading to his shift
after twenty breathless lengths of crawl
and not a sign that he aligned with sad and sorry grifters
like Tommeh, Katie, James,
and all the other Paypal patriots
who ask for cash while making videos
to show you how much hate they've got.
I didn't delve into his proclivities
for folk with wangs or ones with wombs
ask if he had a partner, two, or three
and who did what and how to whom
I don't know if he followed mohammed or buddha or jesus
or if he believed that when we are dead
we all ascend to heaven or just cease to exist
no, none of that entered my head

I shouted *Oi! Fella! You've dropped your hat!*
and he said *Thanks, mate. I'd have lost that.*

**after years of putting her down john
bull kicks europa out of his house and
embraces a bright new future where he
makes his own rules.**

Monday.
and John shrugs his shoulders
says it's been coming for a while
plenty more fish out there, you know
another lager, landlord! smiles
slides money over the bar
breathes deep and crows of freedom
sinks the pint, again again again.

Tuesday.
he's back down the pub
telling anyone who's there
that he's fine without her
no more gip about leaving
the toilet seat up
no earache when he has
a harmless daytime tipple
he's living the dream, people!
you saps should try it.

Wednesday:
she needs him more than he needs her
you'll see, she'll be back, the bitch,
mark his words
crawling on her fucking knees.

Thursday:
pissed, he mutters about betrayal
shoots dark glances round the bar
asks for the loan of a tenner
till, well... whenever
you learn who your friends are
someone helped her take the bloody sofa
yer bastards, you lot, bastards.

Friday:
she's been seen walking out
with another fella on her arm
looking good, someone says
before they're shushed to silence
and they all try to pretend
they can't hear the sound
of a proud man lost
and sobbing in the toilets.

the drunken Polish labourer, homesickness, and the 529

if there is god thinks Piotr
then this bus will not stop
at *sentchiles sick tempull*
places which he cannot name
places which all look the same
bus will not leave him in darkness
on dog-shit chip-box puddle pavement
cold flat waiting

if there is god, bus will drive through night
head south, east through towns
villages neon cities lit by rain
will fall silent only on boat, engine cooling
Piotr will swig at beer through sunrise
turn up music on his phone
see *autobahn* and *kirche*
from top deck front seat window

if there is god
bus will deliver him to dark bread,
barszcz, kielbasa, kopytka,
wódka, wódka, wódka
Piotr gazes out into blur of *noo slain*
knows bus will deliver him home

if there is god
if there is fockin god

Enough

And so, it comes.
That winter morning when you wake
and find that you have had   enough.

You will give it up, you tell yourself,
retreat to the hills, the coast,
a cottage, a boat, a hut
some place out on the edge of it all.
Anywhere but here.
Anything but this.
You make plans to see out your days
walking beaches
scattering resting gulls
climbing mountains
to stare at far horizons.
You tell yourself
you will tend vegetables
grow old by the heat of a fire
lose yourself in books
and the view from a window.

Let the rich and the furious
have the world for themselves.
Much good may it do them.

There's no shame, you tell yourself,

in howling your grief
into the roaring wind
at the stars, the moon,
anything that listens,
in finding solace in the bottle
or the bottom of a pint.
There's no shame in walking
away from the fight,
throwing the towel in.

Just let the rich and the furious
have the world for themselves.
And much good may it do them.

You tell yourself all of this and more.
You even believe it.

And then, one day, it comes.
That morning which has always
been written into your bones
woven into your future
that morning when you wake
and find that you have had

Basta!
Enough!

and you roll up your sleeves
and set to once more.

you do not listen

you do not listen to the radio any more
you do not listen to the radio any more
because standing in the kitchen screaming
obscenities at John Humphrys at 7 o'clock
in the morning isn't the fun it once was
because you have run out of obscenities
because the neighbours have run out of patience
and the police have given you a warning
about disturbing the peace   again

you do not listen to the radio any more
because infotainment is not news
because you really couldn't give a flying one
about Harry, Meghan, or Little Lord Fauntleroy
about Prince Alabaster or Lady Eugenics
(usual caveats, lovely people etc etc blah blah blah)
but you do care that we're paying £2.4m
to refurbish their 'cottage' when finding resources
to replace inflammable cladding is like pulling fucking teeth
and if the royal correspondent ever took time off
from trumpeting the new feudalism
from their forelock-tugging fawning tone of voice
from being a pure embarrassment to hear
if they ever took time off to report *that* loud and clear
you'd give thanks for the miracle,

                                   but they don't

you do not listen to the radio any more
because infotainment is not news
because feeding middle england
their daily frisson of fear is not news
because thought for the sodding day
because if you wanted to listen to
an audio edition of the Daily Mail
you would sign up for an audio edition
of the Daily Mail and it'll be a cold day in hell
before that happens and even then

                            it won't

you do not listen to the radio any more
because infotainment is not news
because once, just once, you'd like them
to interrupt these clichés about knife crime
to head over to Laura Kuenssberg
who is reporting live from the scene of
the sharp end of austerity
the closed-down shuttered-up youth club
the just-axed bus route the zero-hours job
the food bank the food bank the food bank
What's it like there, Laura?
because they wouldn't know how to ask
JohnsonMoggFarageGove a tough question
if their lives depended on it
because speaking truth unto power, folks,
speaking truth unto power

you do not listen to the radio any more
because infotainment is not news
because their knowing world-weariness
does nothing to change anything
is intended to do nothing to change anything
because you are bored of their faux outrage
sick of them asking all the wrong questions
tired of their business as usual
because they will discuss the postcode lottery
without ever mentioning that it isn't a lottery at all
but institutionalised structural violence
but institutionalised structural violence

you do not listen to the radio any more
you don't know what to do with the silence

you think you'll get a dog

Glass collector

Let us sing of the mouse-quiet collector
of glasses, clearer of plates, wiper of tables,
he who returns sauce bottles to their
allotted place on the worktop
he who takes no space at all
asks no space at all
who is seventeen
who will surprise you by butting into
your conversation about the Milky Way
with an extensive knowledge of cosmology
who will shrug and say he taught himself
because what else is there to do here
really, what else is there to do?
Let us sing of the mouse-quiet collector
of glasses, his slow orbit round tables,
of sauce bottles and wisdom
and no space at all.
Let us raise our glasses.
Let us sing.

Karaoke at the Horse & Jockey

Tuesday evening, half past six
and Carole is singing. Again.
Right now, she's hitting the sweet spot
where the vodka and cokes
and the years of desperation
reach a fragile truce, a balance
which will tip, sooner or later,
into fists and fights, or tears.

But now,
      now,
           now...

                        Carole is at the mic
bawling out her tune,
the song she always murders
after a day spent on the booze.
The disco light is flashing blue
green red across flaking walls
and ancient artex, and Carole is
howling out her hope, her pain.

She did it last Tuesday, she'll
do it again next week like as
not, sprinkle herself in market-stall
stardust, council house dreams.

She's the karaoke screeching queen
believing in herself for just as long
as the music lasts, telling anyone
who looks like they might listen

I... will always love... you...oo-oo...

And for these few minutes
she could be anyone.

The poet, the property developer, and the Victorian walled garden

Awestruck, reverent,
clad in cast-iron confidence
you show me the spreadsheet
handed down to you by the gods of commerce,
the natural undeniable laws of finance,
of profit – which is yours
and loss – which is not.

I say you have not calculated the tumble
of chittering goldfinch
as they drop through the branches
to gorge on nijer seed
that you have failed to account for
the joy of the young dog fox
as he basks in the sunshine and listens
for worms burrowing beneath the grass
I ask where the figures are for
the sound of the summer breeze
through trees in leaf, the timelessness,
the dropping away of cares,
how you have valued the soothing of the soul,
and the sense of belonging.

You frown
point to formulas proving the solidity

of bricks and mortar
a world where the acrobatic splendour
of the newly-fledged family of blue tits
and the dancing helix of butterflies
courting in the sunlight
counts for nothing, does not exist.
The trees? You have allowed for them, you say.
See here, the column for
'products, timber', 'woodpulp, optional'
outlay minimal: chainsaw, chipper, tree surgeon
short-term investment, quick return.
There's no arguing with the bottom line, you tell me,
gathering up your papers
sliding them safe into your folder
slipping back into the comfort
of your air-conditioned car.

No arguing at all. None whatsoever.

Later, as you settle into your evening
with a generous glass of wine, wall-sized TV
swill the red and shake your head
at such unexpected, unwarranted sentimentality
over a prime site
as you sink into the leather sofa
switch channels to a sitcom
re-run canned laughter *ha ha ha*
and call it a night
as you climb to bed and set the alarm

I will be making plans, calling
charm after charm after charm.
By the time you wake I'll have smuggled
the song and the beauty of goldfinch
into every last beat of your feathery, fluttering heart.

on that day

when we can barely hear ourselves think
for the pealing of church bells
the cheering of crowds
when all the pubs are full
and the street parties last
till every bottle's empty
and the sun is crawling over the rooftops
for the third time

when we wake on strangers' sofas
on buses and in parks
face down on tables in the kitchen
of houses in towns at the
              other end   of the country
clutching the keys to someone else's car
with no idea how we got there
praying to god for alka-seltzer
muttering we'll never drink again

then
we'll know we were there
wherever it was
whoever we were with
whatever it was we did
(or didn't do)
on that day

that blessed day
when Donald Trump learned to love himself

not
the late-at-night-behind-closed-doors self-loving
in front of the laptop
not the live-streamed-from-a-Moscow-hotel-room
self-loving
where the girls do that thing he loves
make the right encouraging noises
and never draw attention
to his tiny desperate hands

no
not that
cast that image from your mind

seriously
cast it further

on that day
that happy day
the stars and the planets find some new alignment
butterflies flutter in joyful formation
over the last patch of rainforest
and the gods of all the major religions
pause from their eternal game of paintball
shrug their shoulders
decide to toss us a bone

and so it is
on that glorious day
locked in the bathroom with his morning stink
Donnie pauses before the mirror
as he washes his hands
and sees for the first time ever

not the coward who dodged the draft
not the braggard who has no friends
not the mediocre businessman
propped up by daddy's money
not the misogynist who lacks the balls
to make amends
not the climate-change denier
not the birther
not the racist
not the instinctive hapless liar
who tweets bullshit with no basis
not Putin's little puppet
not the purveyor of fake news
not the most inadequate of presidents
unable to fill others' shoes

instead
he sees the lost child he once was
the dreams he once harboured
the readiness to see the best in others
the happiness and innocence and hope
and Donald drops to his knees

by the toilet bowl and sobs
among the splash stains and the soap
picks up his phone and types

I AM SO FUCKING SORRY.

and all across the planet
the party starts
seven billion people giving it large
on the terrestrial dancefloor
pensioners necking more booze
than you could ever shake their stick at
gangsters loved up on pills and purple hearts

on day two, things got so crazy
we even let Theresa May join in
and as the pair of us sat round a fire
doing tequila slammer
after tequila slammer
after tequila slammer
after tequila slammer
with the stars twinkling overhead
she took another crafty toke

and said

comrade, be realistic
about what this does
and doesn't mean

– I leaned in to hear her
above the din of marching bands –

*let's not forget
it's one very small step*

but it's still bigger than his tiny hands.

a poem examining the sociological implications of the now famous incident at Wolverhampton swimming baths involving the slamming of a locker and the dropping of a hat, an incident related here by your narrator who – like all of us – is caught up in a relentlessly acquisitive, materialistic and individualistic culture which sets us at each others' throats and threatens the continued existence of life on this planet we call home

As his beanie hit the floor
I thought *You twat!*
If no-one else has noticed
I'm having that.

A barbarian's response

And then he says to me – without so much as a by your leave – that he'd like a prose poem. A prose poem, if you please! Did you ever hear the like? So I says to him A prose poem, is it? What's one of those when it's at home? He looks at me quare like, because no jumped-up barbarian from the wastelands – that's meself, in this scenario, if you hadn't gathered – has a right to question him. You see, questioning leads to insubordination and we can't be having that. He raises his eyebrows up to heaven, sighs, tells me *A. Prose. Poem.* like it's obvious, clear as day even to an eejit like meself. And that's it, me dander's up. There's red, and I'm seeing it. I take a good gulp of the black stuff, square me shoulders, and let rip. Tell me, smartarse, I says, jabbing my finger at him, tell me how your prose poem is any different from a well-crafted flash fiction, or a shite one. Tell me why it's not a short story. Tell me that. Does he have an answer? Does he bollocks. Just sits there, blank and blinking. And that's how I leave him, mouth opening and shutting and opening again while he tries to get a handle on what happened, and he can stick his prose poem up his corduroy-trousered – A pint, you say? That's very kind. I shouldn't, but go on, I will. The same again. Good man, yerself. I'm gasping.

the whisper was that this was a great film

a legendary film, a film with that great actor
a film with *that scene with butter*
and it was an arthouse film,
set in France,
and there were going to be tits.

It was a film showing for one night only
at the tiny cinema just down the road
and it was after the pubs shut
so we could have a skinful
and stagger in.

The place was packed.
Whether that was down to the great actor,
the butter, or the legendary nude scenes
in the legendary film
I wouldn't like to say.

We slipped into the last two seats
and waited for tits and butter.
Waited for twenty minutes
while the great actor waffled on
and on and on and on.

And on.

Whaddyathink? I whispered
praying to god she wasn't keen
Her reply? *It's fuckin shite!*
Come back to mine, I've margarine.

We upped and left. A belter of a night.

In Which No.45 Once Again Seeks Validation To Dispel The Existential Fear That Gnaws At His Very Soul

Thursday, 4am. The president wakes
Reaches, half-conscious, for his phone
Unwilling, untutored, unable to fight.
Must! Have! Attention! Now!
Punches the keypad over and over

In a desperate, infantile frenzy. Then:
Send.

America! The best! My big red button!

Falls back against the pillow, spent,
Useless, lost. Needing some kind of
Consolation, he mutters that he's bigly
King, in his own mind at least. But
We see the emperor naked, unmanned,
Impeachment barrelling relentless down the line.
The end will be fast.

in the build-up to the sexual act, Trevor's bubbling excitement does battle with his catholic guilt

it was right, it was wrong,
it was fun, it was sin, it
was over and done with
in less than a minute.

impulse

She's standing at the checkout
clutching two bars of chocolate
and she only came in to buy a paper
so she could sit and do the crossword
in the cafe on the corner
before she goes to watch a film.

And now she's got two bars of chocolate
and she's holding them tight.

She tells herself it's because it's cold outside
because the wind would whip the skin
from your face as soon as look at you,
leave you shivering and raw
because the sun is going down
and the last of the light
might look beautiful – to poets –
but the temperature is dropping like a stone
and that means you need a little treat
a little something packed with
cocoa, sugar, energy, and fat.
A little something like two bars of chocolate
the ones she's holding tight.

She knows all about the slick marketing campaigns
run by bright young things from agencies

who applaud themselves for knowing
everything there is to know
about the importance of stocking the product
at eye level
in arms' reach
near the till
to maximise the impulse buy

her impulse buy.

The impulse buy of two bars of chocolate
held tight as she shuffles forward in the queue.

She knows, too, that her therapist would say
It's got a lot to do with guilt, hasn't it, Theresa?
That hand-me-down guilt passed on in the milk
from mother to daughter to daughter
an unwanted heirloom she ought to learn to ditch
and she also knows she's reading way too much
into a 50p bar of chocolate
and its friend, the other 50p bar of chocolate
(both on special offer)
but that's her all over, thinks Theresa, her all over.

She pays. The bars of chocolate slip
into her coat pocket, with the change
and she's outside once more, in the slicing wind
the icy rain, the slanting sleet. Theresa shrinks
down into her coat, walks along the street.

She drops one of the bars into the lap of the girl
folded small under her blanket in the doorway
and if some of the change falls with it
well, Theresa isn't counting.

The other she gives to the guy
who's dancing to his own beat
who's cheering himself on
a big man, light on his feet
unfocussed light in his eyes
who takes the bar, nods
studies it for messages from god
never stops moving
never stops moving.

Two bars of chocolate.

She knows himself would say
Ach, love, it's only a futile gesture
tell her how, in the face of cuts
the absence of a co-ordinated housing strategy
and the ongoing brutality of austerity
two bars of chocolate don't amount to a hill of beans.
And he'd be right. Theresa knows that.

She's not stupid.

But she remembers her mom
singing rebel songs behind the kitchen door

the smell of the fry-up
the taste of fresh bread
all the unspoken words that forever stayed unsaid
and yes, handing out 50p bars
in the dying twilight in a tattered town
may be a gesture
may be futile
but she will always be
her mother's child

and giving others food
is the only way she knows
to say

I love you.

when it happens

and they scrape me off the road
or the morning comes when you find me
cold in bed, sleeping forever
when they shovel me, one of hundreds,
into a pit as the pandemic takes hold,
when – perhaps – I finally fall silent,
mug of coffee in hand, while venting
my spleen about corruption and greed,
Brexit, the politics of bitterness and hate,
my background chunter which comes
as natural as breathing

when that happens, then know this:
I've gone nowhere

and when the sly-eyed fox slinks past your campfire,
or the scent of blossom drifts in through
your open springtime window,
whenever goldfinch chitter in the treetops
or the evening sun fills your eyes with burning gold,
when you hear the call of a buzzard
or the moon is lighting your way home,
and when you see, on a distant hilltop,
the figure of a man striding west along the ridge,
dog bounding beside him

then know I'm there, grinning,
the world is as it should be,
I am spinning around you.

If you want more poems, blogs,
and news of what I'm up to,
pop along to the website:

stevepottinger.co.uk

notes on some of the poems in this book

trainspotting, 1832: The young Princess Victoria famously travelled through the Black Country by train. She didn't like what she saw, and drew the curtains.

the folk who read the news: all about invisible walls, class, privilege, and expectation. With a video on Youtube.

On hearing of the financial difficulties...: Katie Hopkins can't go bankrupt often enough, in my opinion.

Desaparecida: last year a friend and his colleague working in Mexico were abducted, beaten, and assaulted by members of a cartel. They were set free after four long days, but are still recovering from their ordeal. Over 26,000 other people have gone missing at the hands of drug cartels, the police, and state authorities who often work with them.

Mothers' Day: we all know pubs like this, don't we?

welcoming the brave new world... : sunlit uplands, my arse.

universal credit   *individual pain*: official quotes are taken from statements by then Employment Minister Alok Sharma, DWP minister Esther McVey, and DWP literature. Statements in italics are by claimants, and are taken from a Rowntree Foundatin report, as well as articles in The Guardian and Metro newspapers.

the drunken Polish labourer: inspired by a late-night bus journey back from Wolverhampton with Piotr, or someone very like him. St Giles, Sikh Temple, and Noose Lane are all stops on the 529 bus route.

Enough: written on December 13th, 2019. Nuff said.

you do not listen: you write a poem, and three weeks later-John Humphrys announces his retirement. The power of poetry, eh?

Glass collector: a genuine conversation in the **Mothers' Day** pub. Because the Black Country is full of surprises.

on that day: it'll be one hell of a party, won't it? Birthers are conspiracy theorists who believe President Obama wasn't born in the US. The current incumbent of the White House is one of them.

the whisper was that this was a great film: it really wasn't.

In Which No.45 Once Again...: this is an acrostic, btw.

impulse: it's the 21st c. We're living in one of the wealthiest countries in the world. Yet every town needs a Theresa or two. We should be doing better than this, shouldn't we?
A video of ths poem is on Youtube.

there's always a bonus poem....

just turn the page.

Tipton Jedi

at her terminal in the library
of a small, forgotten planet

she wonders who the others are
and how they made it here

when it closes, she walks to the stop
finds the 42 left a long, long time ago

sees the young girl chattering on her mobile
hair up, *Princess* sequinned on her T

the warrior monk striding to the bookie's
firm hold on a can of *Tysker* and his staffie

and the delivery driver who steers his truck
through a hold-your-breath gap

as the school crossing lady parts afternoon
traffic with her lightsaber lollipop

he's a heart-stopping whisker from disaster
grins, drops his payload, motors on

when the bus comes, she boards
for the far-off galaxy of West Brom

and a date with a man who claims
he'll take her places, has a pal

who knows a Wookiee or two, gal
she stares through the bus window

passes the young lad as he downs another pint
tries to get his head around the news about his father

In the 2011 census, fifteen people in Tipton put their religion as 'Jedi'

Ignite Books is a small, independent publisher. This book is the latest in our series which we hope puts thought-provoking, entertaining writing before a new audience. We have a lot of fun doing this, but we also survive on a shoestring budget and a lot of graft. So, if you've enjoyed this book, please tell your friends about us. You can also find us on twitter, so drop by and say hallo. And to learn more about what we do, or to shop for our other publications, you'll find our website at **ignitebooks.co.uk**

Thank you.